Tickets!

Written by Alice Hemming

Illustrated by Mike Byrne

Collins

Trish packs a travel bag for her trip.

The ticket man needs to stamp her ticket.

Trish checks the pockets of
her sundress.

7

Trish checks her panda lunchbox.

It is a crisp sandwich for lunch.

Crunch!

9

Did she stash it with her flip flops? No!

The man offers to sell Trish a ticket.

Trish hunts for her credit card in her handbag.

13

Ticket

 Review: After reading

Use your assessment from hearing the children read to choose any GPCs, words or tricky words that need additional practice.

Read 1: Decoding

- Ask the children:
  - Can you think of any words that rhyme with **stamp**? (e.g. *damp, lamp, ramp, camp*)
  - Can you think of any words that rhyme with **stuck**? (e.g. *luck, duck, truck*)

Read 2: Prosody

- Model reading each page with expression to the children. Have fun using different voices to read the speech bubbles.
- After you have read each page, ask the children to have a go at reading with expression.

Read 3: Comprehension

- Turn to pages 14 and 15 and ask the children to retell the story using the pictures for support.
- For every question ask the children how they know the answer. Ask:
  - What items does Trish pack in her bag? (e.g. *a teddy, a camera, a teapot, a ball*)
  - Where do you think she is going? (e.g. *on holiday*)
  - How do you think the ticket man is feeling? (e.g. *annoyed, cross, angry, mad, frustrated*)
  - Where did Trish find her ticket? (*in her handbag*)
  - What would she have had to do if she hadn't found the ticket? (*buy another one*)